Milly, M[...]
and
Mipper

"We may look different but we feel the same."

Mipper owned a motorcycle with a sidecar
for two.

Every day, she strapped on her helmet and
buckled her boots.

"Milly and Molly," she said. "I must have fresh air."

"We must too," Milly and Molly agreed.

"Well, what are we waiting for?" asked Mipper,
delighted.

They rode by the suburbs through lavender and lilac.

They rode down the lanes through
buttercups and bluebells

Mipper smiled and breathed deeply, her nose held high.

They rode by the farmland through haystacks and heather.

They rode down the avenues through
mushrooms and moss.

Mipper smiled and breathed deeply, her
nose held high.

They rode by the streams through ferns
and forget-me-nots.

And they rode down to the coast
through salty, sea air.

Mipper came to a halt. She would go no further.

"Milly and Molly," she said. "This is fresh air."

"We think so too," Milly and Molly agreed.

Mipper took off her boots and her helmet too.
"Something's not right," she thought
to herself.

She sifted her toes through the grainy, warm sand.

She smiled and breathed deeply, her nose
held high.

"I know what's not right," Mipper thought to herself. She strapped on her helmet and buckled her boots.

"Milly and Molly," she said. "We must take care of the air. Fresh air is a must. So tomorrow it's out with the motorcycle and in with our bicycles."

"We can do that," Milly and Molly agreed.

They rode all the way home and sang as they went.

"Take care of the air, fresh air is a must."